Foreword

A delightful way to learn history through the eyes of the magnificent ravens of the Tower of London.

It brings the Tower's history to life through the ages.

Chris Skaife, Tower Ravenmaster.

ISBN 978-1-5272-8348-0

   MarkOzworls

We Present

A History of

The Tower of London

By those who were there from the start

The Ravens

We were here many years before the Normans and even before the Anglo-Saxons. We always tried to be friendly with our human neighbours. But, unfortunately we always seemed to appear on their doorstep just before somebody died.

One day everything changed when the invading Normans
arrived and ordered everyone to build a big Tower,
or keep, for the new king. The two Normans here are
showing how big they want it to be.

Everybody had to work on the building of the Tower. They complained that they couldn't return home to plough the fields to grow food. Some stones for the Tower were even brought all the way from Normandy.

After twenty years of work the Tower was finished.
It was the biggest, tallest, building anyone, or any
raven had ever seen. The side which faced the river
was ninety feet high.

In **1100**, soon after the Tower was finished, a man named Ranulf Flambard, the Bishop of Durham, was imprisoned in one of the turrets. One night he got his guards drunk on wine and, holding his bishops crozier, climbed out of the Tower and escaped.

In the **1190's**, while the King, Richard I, was away on crusade the Tower was looked after by a man named William Longchamp who was the Bishop of Ely.
He wanted to improve the Tower's defences so he ordered a big ditch, or moat, to be dug around it.

His plan was to use the water from the River Thames to fill the moat. However, because the river is tidal it failed to flood properly and was little more than a muddy ditch. We also pointed out that any bird could just fly across it.

King Richard's successor was not very good. In fact he
was known as Bad King John. In 1216 the barons
rebelled against him and took control of the Tower.
They invited Prince Louis of France to be King. He
stayed here at the Tower where the French knights
complained about the lack of wine and having to drink
English beer.

We never got a French king because when King John died the barons supported his son, King Henry III. In **1240** the new King Henry ordered the building of a new 'noble gateway' to the west of the castle. Then, on St. George's Day, his newly built tower collapsed.

The King's noble gateway was rebuilt more soundly this time. Then, as predicted to a priest by the ghost of the murdered Archbishop of Canterbury, Thomas Beckett, the tower collapsed again. This time irreparably.

King Henry also decided to have the Tower painted.
In March **1240** gallons of Whitewash was brought to the
Tower and work began. As you will understand we ravens,
being proud of our black plumage, stayed well out of the
way until the now White Tower was finished.

King Henry didn't have much success with his western entrance but he did oversee the building of the inner wall. He also saw the growth of the Tower Menagerie which included lions, an elephant, and even a polar bear.

In **1244** a Welsh prince called Gruffydd ap Llywelyn
tried to copy Flambard and escape from the White
Tower. Unfortunately, he was a big man and his self made
rope broke sending him to his death. When they found his
body the next morning, they couldn't find his head which
had snapped back between his shoulder blades.

The growth of the Tower continued between 1275 and 1280 when the new King, Edward I, decided that he wanted another wall built around it. The land for it had to be taken from the river at low tide. We would warn the workmen when the tide was coming in.

King Edward I's work on the Tower included a new moat. This was supervised by a man called Master Walter who had come all the way from Holland. The new moat was wider than the old one and stayed full of water, although we could still fly across it.

King Edward I's new wall included a new riverside apartment. This was called St. Thomas' Tower after St. Thomas Beckett. However, during his thirty five year reign, King Edward only spent fifty three days here at the Tower. The riverside entrance is now known as Traitors' Gate.

By now the Tower was the biggest castle in the land, and in **1279** a Royal Mint for the manufacture of coins was established. Gold and silver bullion would arrive from ships on the river. The work was noisy and dangerous so we stayed out of the way.

Then, in 1303, following an attempted theft from
Westminster Abbey, the Great Wardrobe which
contained all the Kings precious and valuable objects,
including the Crown Jewels, was brought to the
Tower for safe keeping.

One night in December **1340** King Edward III turned up unannounced at the Tower and was able to walk in unchallenged. We did try to stop him but the poor security led him to introduce what has become known as the Ceremony of the Keys.

King Edward was worried about security because he had started a war with France which was to last over 100 years. The Tower played host to the French King, Jean LeBon, who had been captured in 1357. He stayed in the White Tower with his court, servants and his jester, the hugely entertaining Master John The Fool.

The cost of the ongoing war saw the introduction of a new Poll Tax. In June 1381 the peasants of south-east England revolted against it and London was attacked. The young King, Richard II, met the rebels to hear their complaints. Later, when the rebels leader was killed, he said that he would be their captain.

While the King was away a group of peasants broke into the Tower. They ran through the buildings stealing weapons, searching for Simon of Sudbury who had introduced the detested Poll Tax. They found him praying in the chapel in the White Tower.

They dragged him and his associate Robert Hales out of the Tower and up on to Tower Hill, where they hacked him to pieces, before putting his head on a pole and carrying it to London Bridge

Tower Hill where Sudbury and Hales were killed came
to be used as a place for executions. In 1465 King
Edward IV had a permanent scaffold erected there.
For us ravens it was a great place to go and scavenge
especially after an execution.

Today the only things we scavenge are any unguarded sandwiches, ham and beef are particular favourites, and whatever we can recycle from the dustbins around the Tower. We also like a nibble on the occasional finger so watch out.

Edward IV had his scaffold erected during the War of the Roses between the Houses of York and Lancaster. In **1471** his rival for the throne, King Henry VI, was imprisoned in the Tower. On **21**st May that year he was 'stykked with a dagger' whilst at prayer in the Wakefield Tower. Some say it was by the King's brother, Richard the Duke of Gloucester.

In **1478** the King's other brother, George the Duke of Clarence, was accused of plotting against him and found guilty of treason. He was brought to the Tower and executed by being drowned in a vat of wine.

When Edward IV died in **1483** his son became King Edward V. He was only twelve years old and was looked after here at the Tower with his brother by their uncle Richard. We would visit them to play but one day they just disappeared.

Uncle Richard became King Richard III but he was killed by Henry Tudor at the Battle of Bosworth in **1485** when he couldn't find a horse. Henry Tudor then crowned himself as King Henry VII.

King Henry VII united the Houses of York and Lancaster by marrying Elizabeth of York. She later died here at the Tower and her body was put in the chapel in the White Tower so people could come and see it and say goodbye.

King Henry VII's son and successor King Henry VIII oversaw an improvement of the defences at the Tower, including the installation of new cannons, and the development of the armoury in the White Tower and elsewhere.

As well as new weapons and armour Henry also liked
having new wives. Unfortunately, like many people
with new things, he sometimes lost or discarded them.
Most sadly, his second and fifth wives, Anne Boleyn
and Catherine Howard, whom he had executed here
at the Tower.

King Henry VIII's divorce from his first wife, Catherine of Aragon, and establishment as Head of the Church of England was opposed by many, including Sir Thomas More who was imprisoned in the Tower from 1534 until his execution in July 1535.

The death of King Henry VIII's son and heir Edward VI in 1553 saw a young lady named Lady Jane Grey spend nine days as Queen, before the throne was claimed by King Henry's daughter, Mary. Poor Lady Jane would later meet her end here at the Tower.

Following the Thomas Wyatt rebellion against Queen Mary I her half-sister, Elizabeth, was imprisoned in the Tower in March 1554. We would see her trying to catch a glimpse of her favourite courtier, Robert Dudley, as she walked on the wall between the Bell and Beauchamp Towers.

After Queen Mary's death Elizabeth became Queen Elizabeth I. She feared a Catholic invasion of England and used a network of spies to find those plotting against her. She had many people imprisoned and tortured here at the Tower.

Philip Howard, the Earl of Arundel, for example, spent
ten years imprisoned in the Beauchamp Tower under
sentence of death solely for being a Catholic peer.
He was kept company by a dog which visited him and,
of course, the ravens.

Another prisoner was a Jesuit priest named Father John Gerard who, in 1597, made a daring escape from the Cradle Tower. Rumour has it he went to Europe and joined a Catholic plot against the crown.

That plot led, in 1605, to Guy Fawkes being found
under the Houses of Parliament with barrels of
gunpowder. He was planning to blow up King James I.
We stood guard whilst he was questioned and
tortured on the rack. Not surprisingly, he confessed
and was executed.

The famous explorer Sir Walter Raleigh was imprisoned for thirteen years in the Bloody Tower for plotting against James I. While he was there he started writing A History Of The World. We don't know if he finished it before he was executed in 1618.

A new threat to the monarchy erupted in **1642** when
the King, Charles I, had one argument too many with
his Parliament. England descended into Civil War
between the forces of Parliament, under Oliver
Cromwell, and those loyal to the King.

London and the Tower came under the control of the forces of Parliament. They stationed a garrison of soldiers here from their army. They were referred to as 'round-heads' because of the shape of their helmets.

After the end of the Civil War in **1649**, and the execution
of King Charles I, Parliament ordered that the Crown
Jewels be sold or melted down to make coins. Then,
in **1660**, the monarchy was restored under King Charles II
and a new set of Crown Jewels had to be made.

Meanwhile, the man who had been in charge at the Tower before the restoration, Sir John Barkstead, was rumoured to have buried £7000 of gold and silver somewhere in the grounds. After his execution many people, including Samuel Pepys, tried in vain to search for it.

Samuel Pepys also watched the Great Fire of 1666 from the tower of the nearby All Hallows church. We retreated to the top of the White Tower. In hindsight this wasn't a very good idea as it was being used at the time to store barrels of gunpowder.

On the 9th May 1671 a 'Colonel' Thomas Blood and his accomplices tried to steal the Crown Jewels. Luckily, we ravens and the son of the Keeper of the Jewels arrived just in time and the thieves were stopped. Astonishingly Blood was then pardoned by the King.

Some labourers were doing some work on the stairs in
the chapel in the White Tower in 1674 when they
found a box. When it was opened it was found to
contain the remains of two young boys. The King said
they must be the bodies of the two princes who had
gone missing.

In 1675, a scientist named John Flamsteed, briefly installed an Observatory in the north-east turret of the White Tower. He complained to the King, Charles II, that we weren't helping with his work and demanded that we be removed.

The King was told about an old legend that if we left the Tower the monarchy would fall and the Tower would crumble to dust. He declared that there should always be at least six ravens kept at the Tower and Mr. Flamsteed and his Observatory were sent down the river to Greenwich.

The famous scientist Sir Isaac Newton was Warden and then Master of the Mint from 1698 until 1727. He thought of putting an inscription on the coins to stop people clipping the edges for the metal. We ravens don't like things being clipped either but sometimes it has to be done.

In 1714 we got another new Royal Family with the arrival of the Hanoverians from Germany. The new German King, George I, spoke very little English and referred to us as 'die raben'. The Middle Tower was refaced with his coat of arms in 1717. We helped of course.

Supporters of the old Royal Family, known as Jacobites, rebelled. In 1716 one of them, Earl Nithsdale, escaped from the Tower disguised in a change of his wife's clothing. We felt sorry for the guards as it is also very difficult to tell men and lady ravens apart.

In **1745** the Jacobites rebelled again and the last public beheading on Tower Hill, that of Simon Fraser the Lord Lovat, took place on 9th April **1747**. He was so old that he had to be carried through the crowd to the scaffold on a chair.

Even after the Tower Menagerie closed in the 1830's people still came to try to see the animals. One popular event which first took place in 1698 was the 'Washing Of The Lions'. This would take place occasionally on the 1st April.

The Tower Menagerie was closed on the orders of the Constable, the Duke of Wellington. In **1843** he also ordered the draining of the moat which had become awfully smelly and full of disease. You wouldn't believe the things we found in there.

The opening of the Tower to the public led to the hiring of an architect, Sir Anthony Salvin, to restore it to a more 'medieval' style. Despite our offers of assistance, he, and his successor, John Taylor, got carried away and knocked down some important remains.

The Tower became more and more popular as a tourist attraction with people coming to see the historic sites, the Crown Jewels and of course the ravens. Of course as the custodians of the Tower we were always very welcoming.

In **1897** soldiers from across the British Empire gathered at the Tower to prepare for Queen Victoria's Diamond Jubilee celebrations. Some of them had to camp in the moat which was easier now that it had been drained.

In **1914** the Tower was again filled with soldiers. This time recruits preparing to go and fight in the Great War. During the war the Tower was used to imprison and execute enemy spies. Through it all the Tower remained open to the public.

When war broke out again in 1939, we knew that as
symbols of British resistance, both us and the Tower
would be targets for the enemy. To help defend the
Tower we helped out as unofficial 'spotters' during
the Blitz on London.

As the bombing increased, we left the Tower along with London's children, to go to somewhere safer. But don't worry, we hadn't forgotten about the legend of the Tower and the ravens, so at least one of us stayed behind to look after the place.

The Tower moat was turned into a giant allotment to grow vegetables as part of the Dig for Victory campaign. Ravens don't really like vegetables but we helped where we could. Although it has to be said we do like burying and digging things up.

When the war finished in **1945** we found that some parts of the Tower, including the Old Hospital Block and the North Bastion had been damaged or destroyed.

Although the war was over young men still had to do
National Service. In 1952, the soon to be notorious
East-End gangsters, Ronnie and Reggie Kray were
imprisoned in the Tower for refusing to do their National
Service with the Royal Regiment of Fusiliers.

In the **1960's** even though we had been looking after ourselves for centuries, it was decided to give one of the Yeoman Warders the job of taking care of us. He is called the Yeoman Raven-master. Don't tell anybody; but we also have a Raven Yeoman-master.

In 1974 the Tower once again became a target when terrorists planted a bomb in the basement of the White Tower. It was said to have been the work of the IRA in their violent campaign for Irish unity.

In **1980** raven Grog escaped from the Tower and was found some time later, as his name befits, outside the Rose and Punchbowl pub in the east-end. More recently raven Munin took a trip to Greenwich before being returned to the Tower.

One of the must-see events at the Tower, the first of which took place for Anne Boleyn's Coronation in 1533, is a Gun Salute. These happen on the wharf to mark special occasions such as Royal birthdays and State Visits and are very LOUD.

The Yeoman Warders, or Beefeaters, who were founded back in **1485** by Henry VII as his bodyguard and to guard the Tower, do guided tours. They are almost as popular as the ravens and are a great way to hear the stories in human-speak.

In **2012** the Olympic Games arrived in London, and
the Tower, and of course the ravens, played a
central role. We made sure that the Olympic flame
stayed alight while it was here and looked after
all the medals.

2012 also saw the Queen's Diamond Jubilee. We saluted the Royal Regatta as it sailed past along with the Chief Yeoman Warder and the Constable Of The Tower. Who, we noticed, was wearing a very fetching feathered hat.

In 2014 to mark 100 years since the outbreak of
the First World War, 888,246 ceramic poppies were
planted in the moat. Each one represented a fallen
British or Commonwealth soldier. We thought
about all our feathered friends, such as the carrier
pigeons, who had fallen.

The centenary of the end of the war in **2018** was marked with the installation of thousands of candles in the Tower moat. Each night they would burn bright and then flicker and fade. We would watch until the Raven-master said it was time for bed.

We now have a new generation of ravens growing up at the Tower hungry for food and for history. With them the story of the Tower and of the ravens continues....

To find out more about the Tower and the Ravens visit:

www.hrp.org.uk/toweroflondon

Printed in Great Britain
by Amazon